How Many Legs?

by Norman Platnick

MONDO

Here is a bird.
Is it a bird with one leg?
No. One leg is up.

A bird has two legs.

Here is an elephant.
Is it an elephant with five legs?
No. The trunk is not a leg!

An elephant has four legs.

Here is an ant.
Is it an ant with eight legs?
No. The feelers are not legs!

11

An ant has six legs.

Here is a spider.
Can you see eight legs?
Yes. A spider has eight legs.

Here is a worm.
Can you see legs?
No. A worm has no legs.